the rest
that works

A Little Primer

scott daniels

the rest
that works

A Little Primer

Eau Claire, Wisconsin

ISBN-13: 978-0692414378
ISBN-10: 0692414371
Library of Congress Control Number: 2015936983

RTW Press

Eau Claire, Wisconsin
An Imprint of
Rider Green Book Publishers
North Berwick, Maine

"Are you tired? Worn out? Burned out on religion? Come to me. Get away with me and you'll recover your life. I'll show you how to take a real rest. Walk with me and work with me - watch how I do it. Learn the unforced rhythms of grace. I won't lay anything heavy or ill-fitting on you. Keep company with me and you'll learn to live freely and lightly."

– Matthew 11:28-30 (MSG)

DEDICATION

This book is dedicated to Jesus,
the pioneer and perfecter
of *the rest that works* (Hebrews 12:2).

ACKNOWLEDGEMENTS

There are too many people to list who deserve thanks for *the rest that works,* so I am going to focus on those who helped shape this particular book:

My family starting with my parents: Dan and Betty Daniels, my sister Gay and brother John (who drew the child in God's Hand that sums up *the rest that works* so well). Their love led me into much of the perspective here.

My wife Anita and our kids, Josh, Ben and Bri. They have been my constant mutual explorers. No one could ask for better, more loving people.

My editor, Cynthia Astle, who helped clarify the ideas here.

My friend Kathi West, who asked for this book.

Thanks to all of you for everything.

CONTENTS

INTRODUCTION

This is a sneaky little book.

A friend came up to me after a workshop based on a first draft of *The rest that works*. She said something like, "You have some great zingers that sneak up on a person. I want those zingers pulled out and put into a little book along with the most basic ideas and steps for entering *the rest that works*. I get the need for the big book but a little book like that would be most helpful when I don't have time for a big one."

This primer is an attempt at that little book. It's not really a "best of *the rest that works*" because real-life stories, sacred texts and exercises can lead us into some deep insights, and most importantly, experiences with the Living God. Ultimately, *the rest that works* is about the way we actually live our daily lives, not ideas.

Perspective shapes experience; that's why

there are a lot of perspective-oriented ideas here. If our functioning perspective has been filtering out Divine parts of reality, our experience won't improve until we expand our mindset. That's the main gift of this little primer: making sure that our minds are open, aligned and primed to the reality of the Great I AM -- the Living, Loving God. The big book and other aspects of *the rest that works* ministries offer more extensive, experiential opportunities (there is a list of *the rest that works* materials in the back of this primer and online at therestthatworks.com). If you are interested in pursuing the lifestyle of *the rest that works*, I would highly recommend the big book and those other materials.

For now though, I hope that this little book is sneaky like Jesus' sayings and parables. He pioneered and perfected *the rest that works* and gets the credit for anything helpful here. But just as with his teachings, I would not try to read this book with the goal of figuring it all out in an hour. Better to move slowly and thoughtfully, seeing the ideas here as pointers and openings to explore rather than endpoints or boxes.

More power to you in allowing the Living God to sneak more and more into your life.

Blessings,
Scott

SECTION I
Invitation

"But seek ye first the kingdom of God, and his righteousness; and all these things shall be added unto you."

—Matthew 6:33 (KJV)

A young boy was reading the names on a plaque outside a sanctuary one Sunday morning. The pastor came over and the boy asked, "Who were these people?" The pastor replied somberly, "They died in the service, son." Wide-eyed, the little boy asked, "Which one, the 8:30 or the 10:00 o'clock?" Unfortunately, many people can identify with that little boy (mostly worried about dying of boredom).

A vibrant faith leads us on a loving adventure with the Living God – the Wonderful, Creative Spirit Behind and Within all of Life. I think that most people want a passionate journey with the Great I AM but things keep getting in the way. Fear and other issues often undermine our best attempts at a healthy, adventurous faith.

The rest that works addresses that. It is a method of resting in the Living God and working from there. It is a philosophy of life, faith perspective and mindfulness practice all wrapped into one. It

5

is a way to walk the journey of life by learning to be at home in God's Love like a branch at rest in a vine (John 15).

The Great I AM is striving to secure and lead us lovingly if we are open to cooperating with the Divine in earnest. We can improve our responsiveness by some intentional steps. *The rest that works* brings some key steps together. This is why Jesus said, "Here's what I want you to do: Find a quiet, secluded place so you won't be tempted to role-play before God. Just be there as simply and honestly as you can manage. The focus will shift from you to God, and you will begin to sense his grace" (Matthew 6:6, MSG). It doesn't matter whether we use meditation, prayer, quiet time or even just a walk to be open to God, but we need to be sincere and consistent. Be real and open with God in a way that is true to you. No plastic prayers. No trying to "play God" with God either (no telling God what to do as if we know how the Living God should lead us). The goal here is to learn and live a personal way to open to God's Love on the one hand and branch out creatively with it on the other. That's what *the rest that works* is all about.

The rest that works leaves open blanks here and there. That's part of why God can use it as a guiding practice for your life as you insert things that are true to you. There is a reason that some form of *the rest that works* lies in all of the great spiritual traditions. As our personal relationship with God deepens, we find ourselves more at home wherever we are.

Believe that your Creator loves you and will guide you from where you are. The Living God knows you better than you do, is prepared for you and way ahead of you. Heaven's got a plan to lead you in home-making love, but the journey takes commitment and humility. This is why Jesus brought two contrasting ideas together as foundational:

"Seek ye first the kingdom of God and his righteousness" — and — *"Unless you change and become like little children, you will never enter the kingdom of heaven."*

—Matthew 6:33 (KJV) and 18:3 (NIV)

He was essentially saying: "Fall in love with the Living God like a child again and live that love out with all you've got! Take life seriously and playfully! Lighten up while loving earnestly. You may have to rest regarding some of your assumptions, but the freedom and joy you will find coming home to God and loving with your Creator will be worth it."

Here's a personal example of the kind of invitation home in God's Love that we're talking about: A few years ago I had a significant dream. I was a student in a high school hallway. Other students were walking the halls, oblivious to the fact that there was a light, wispy mist present. As I

7

stared at it, the mist coalesced in front of me. That
threw me a bit but it didn't seem menacing so I
stayed still. A golden key materialized. I reached
for it. It was hot. That caught me off guard. I let go,
but then didn't want it to disappear, so I reached
for it again and put it in my pocket. It cooled there,
but upon grasping it again it grew hot and the
appearance of things around me changed — like
they were becoming a gray background for a more
colorful, unfolding drama. A flame appeared on
the floor that led out of the school. Surprised, I re-
leased the key in my pocket and everything went
back to normal. I had a decision to make. I went
about my day for a while, weighing my options
(still in the dream). While very mysterious, nothing seemed wrong about the key or the flame, and
I wanted to find out where the flame led. So when
I had the chance, I made my way to an open place
in the hallway and grasped the key again. The
heat returned and the line of flame reappeared.
I followed it out of the school. It led me across a
nearby pasture and I found myself walking along
what was essentially a flaming fence. I was a little
scared when I heard a loving motherly voice say,
"It's all right, little lamb." So I prayed, realized
everything was right and kept going, still a little
anxious but not terrified and full of anticipation.
After rounding a couple of hills, the fire line led
to an old farmhouse. It was for sale and I saw a
vision of treasure in the basement. I was invited to

come home to unimaginable riches. It would take work, but it was a priceless opportunity. When I awoke, I felt lots of energy and knew it was an important dream. I felt very loved.

I've often prayed about that dream and have some ideas of what it meant (though there may be more to come). Making a true home in the Love of God takes a complex mix of effort. It takes faith, patience and trust but also desire, passion, courage and commitment. These are all elements of love. This partially explains why Jesus told us to "Love the Lord your God with all your heart, all your soul, all your strength and all your mind." Society's high-school understanding of spirituality does not encourage let alone support such an effort very well, nor do most social evaluations, roles, rules and dramas. One must be willing to leave those things behind to have the treasure. Doing so can be scary for a variety of reasons. But we have tremendous heavenly help if we are willing to follow it.

Now jump ahead to a month ago, while finishing this primer and the big book of *the rest that works*. After some questions from my publisher, I was wondering who the primary audience would be for *the rest that works* – people in traditional churches, people who struggle with the limiting aspects of traditional Christianity, people on the fringe of traditional Christianity . . . I wasn't really sure but could identify with and respect all of

9

them. That night, I found myself entering the old farmhouse of my previous dream from years ago (as described above). I sensed a very loving presence and turned to see a motherly robed figure gently close the door behind me as if to say "Welcome home." I couldn't make her out clearly but realized that she was a powerful spiritual being. The love emanating from her was wonderful. I had a knowing that she was the one who had said, "It's all right, little lamb." Without thinking to ask her name, I asked, "Who is this for?" (meaning *the rest that works* and the journey symbolized in my dream). She looked at me without moving her lips and I heard gently but firmly, "Whoever really wants it." There was no judgment implied of anybody if they didn't want it. It was simply an open invitation for whoever really wanted to make the type of journey home in God's Love that *the rest that works* offers. There was an implicit recognition that there are other valuable paths. She was peaceful and positive, and put me more at home than words can describe. I awoke still not really knowing who she was but wanting to share God's Home-Making Love – the way the woman in my dream did with me, and ultimately the way any of us can once we are at home ourselves in God's Love. I awoke even more committed to offering *the rest that works* as well and as widely as possible.

My hope is that whoever really wants it will have home-making experiences of Divine Love

10

through developing their own form of *the rest that works.* This is my prayer for you (and may it be boredom free).

REST STOP

"The Spirit of God made me what I am, the breath of God Almighty gave me life! God always answers, one way or another."

—Job 33:4 (MSG)

I want your experience of this book to model a form of *the rest that works.* That's why the big book of *the rest that works* is full of rest stops (like this one). To keep this primer short, there are very few formal rest stops. But please take ample breaks while considering the ideas here. Don't force yourself through. That would miss the point.

Let your reflection times move like the ebb and flow of your breath. Breath prayers can lead us into the truth behind Job 32:8 (MSG): ". . . *it's God's Spirit in a person, the breath of the Almighty One, that makes wise human insight possible."*

The rhythm of our breath when we are relaxed harmonizes with the natural, unforced rhythms of God's Grace. Our spirit flows with a pattern of forgiveness and love: Exhaling — letting go and coming to rest, and then inhaling – welcoming inspiring energy to do the work of living the next moment. As we move deeply with this pattern, our bodies can help us sense who and even what we are beyond egocentric thinking. No one is totally independent. (If you think you are, try holding your breath). We all draw upon energy from beyond us in order to keep living. We exist as parts of a divinely created, Loving Flow. Living mindful of that, our sense of connection to the Living, Loving God expands and we start entering *the rest that works* mentally and spiritually – we start living a grateful, loving mindfulness.

Let the Love that created you wash over you, taking any harsh judgments with it. Any needed correction will then be experienced as opportunity and relief rather than punishment. If needed, that is how God's correction comes when we live *the rest that works.*

The Living God and heavenly helpers are on the job. Our job is to trust and learn to work with them. Test for love and then accept whom and what God sends. Stop trying to lead by following the Holy Spirit and those in heaven who know you better than you know yourself. There is relief in that.

If you disagree with something here, please simply disagree with it and reflect on what you think is true, staying open to the Spirit Behind and

Within All of Life. God will work with that even if the Spirit has to work around my errors. Go with what feels right deep within. Move forward when it feels right. God will move with you without forcing you. There is no rush.

The goal of this book

"Say not, 'I have found the path of the soul.' Say rather, 'I have met the soul walking upon my path.' For the soul walks on all paths."

— **Kahlil Gibran,** *The Prophet*

The Bible implies that our souls are breaths of God's Spirit (Genesis 2:7). *The rest that works* is a way to feel for The Spirit on your journey. It's a sail that can be set in any heart. It's an art not a science. Like with all art, basic ideas and techniques can be taught but one's practice, passion and expression are personal. That's good because to mean anything, love must be personal. You can't be in love without the experience really affecting you; if it's not affecting you, you're not really in love.

The rest that works has lovingly led me to inner peace, patience, meaning, passion and joy over time. It has been particularly relevant for me during trying tests in ministry, family life and midlife challenges including two grand mal seizures, five months of bed rest to heal a lumbar puncture, and a serious bout with cancer for our young daugh-

13

ter. *The rest that works* helped me draw from the wellspring of Heavenly Love in those times and beyond them. This isn't pie-in-the-sky stuff. *The rest that works*, works. Sometimes, it's the only thing that works.

Some people have told me that *the rest that works* has changed their lives. That makes my day. But I can tell you without a doubt that they each sought to develop and practice their own form of *the rest that works* over time (at least a few months). They tried things and developed practices that worked for them, making sure that the steps of the cycle were covered in some way. That's when *the rest that works* brought a significant shift for them and their relationship with God became more exciting, meaningful and wonderful. That's not to say that they had everything figured out, but rather just the opposite. They had adventurous, effective faith which brought love from within in the midst of things they couldn't figure out or control (like other people). That's when our lives work best. That is the goal of *the rest that works* – living lives aligned with the best and highest good for ourselves and others through the Love of the Living God.

The Cycle of The Rest that Works

1) Trust the Living God in Whom "we live and move and have our being" with the confidence and playfulness of an adored child—because you are (Acts 17:28).

2) Rest—Relax your critical mind as you open your heart. Slow down, take a few breaths and trust the unforced rhythms of grace that are giving you life. Settle in with them like a branch in a vine.

3) Work—Seek to create the highest good in the moment with the Holy Spirit – the Spirit Who Brings Wholeness through Love – not a critical spirit that would condemn you or others.

SECTION II
Excerpts

"That which makes the most difference is feeling the deep Home-making Love of God, no matter what else we are doing."

This section is an attempt to offer some "sneaky zingers" from the big book, my online blogs and a sermon or two on *the rest that works*. Hopefully, some of these short descriptive thoughts strike a "knowing chord" within you. That's the first step of *the rest that works*: knowing why and how dearly we want to live in the Love of the Living God. We can grow in doing so with God's help. The first step is willingness to believe in a Being greater than ourselves and confidence in the Love giving us life.

Descriptive phrases for *the rest that works* (please pick or create your own):

- resting in God and working from there
- getting to loving with God
- the art of allowing the Living, Loving God
- participating in God's Home-making Love
- Jesus' Way and Truth of Loving with God
- living a life of loving mindfulness with God

19

Here is my favorite personal excerpt describing my most common application of *the rest that works:*

"Things usually go like this for me: I am worried about this or that and running around like a chicken with my head cut off. Then I become aware that I am anxious. It's a feeling of "I better do this or that, or else — (unspoken bottom line) – I won't be loved." That's my trigger to rest, remember God is Love, settle in with the unforced rhythms of Grace giving me life, trust the Living God again, feel for loving leads and work from there. That's *the rest that works.*"

GOD

That which makes the most difference is feeling the deep Home-making Love of God, no matter what else we are doing.

~

Our images of God tend to be too limited and limiting.

~

A lot of people don't feel safe with God. They feel like they're on trial when the word "God" comes up and they get defensive. The Living God's Love doesn't have much chance of getting through.

~

Everyone is already in a relationship with the Living God – the Creative Spirit behind and within all of Life. It's mostly a question of quality – how conscious, connected, open, honest, personal, loving and adventerous is the relationship?

Our Creator is a Living God of second chances.

Depending on how you count, there are from 16 to 102 "names" or images of God in the Bible alone. They are all connected by Love, but each beckons slightly different possibilities.

The Great I AM is a mysterious yet wonderful noun and verb. As chips off the ol' block, so are we.

The images of God in the Bible allow for both expansive breadth and extreme focus. The Living God is experienced in both.

A lot of people don't believe in God because they think God has let them down. An image of God probably did. But I assure you, The Living God didn't.

The possibilities with the Living God are endless.

22

The Great I AM affirms people being free, trying things and making mistakes. Freedom is required for faith that works (because love must be free).

———～—

It takes courage to let God be free.

———～—

Think of the respect the Living God shows us. It takes tremendous respect for a parent to say, "You are completely free. You owe me nothing. You can even ignore me if you want without undermining my deep love for you. You will always have a home with me even if you don't choose to use it."

———～—

The Living God feels great.

———～—

God wants our lives to be love stories. *The rest that works* is a way to write a rich, loving storyline from your heart, day by day, with your Creator. It's a means to take your life well beyond a one-way or shallow relationship with the Living God (and others).

23

"God" includes the love that moves between us.

———～-

Here's what makes *the rest that works*, work: The Great I AM is central to everything. Centering on the Living, Loving God makes sense.

———～-

We get lost to the very degree that we don't align our lives with the Creative Forces of God (whether we are religious or not). In the final analysis, life is as simple and complex as that.

———～-

Cultivating a loving mindfulness takes us into the creative territory of God. The irony is that sometimes we have to rest in order to get there.

———～-

The Living God has an incredible sense of humor as well as patience. Laughter can be very freeing and holy.

Christianity needs to better allow the Mothering Aspect of God. Books like William P. Young's, *The Shack* exemplify helpful re-imaging (where Papa God appears as a black woman and the Holy Spirit appears as a Japanese woman).

To reject images of God is not to reject the Living God, but it is hard not to throw the baby out with the bathwater. Better to be open to a variety of imagery and test for love than thoughtlessly reject imagery that has helped people work with God (sometimes over thousands of years). Let's have humility about this.

God squirms when we try to pin God down with our definitions. Better to humbly let the Living God Be.

BELIEF

Faith in God or Christ is about the belief at work when we turn to someone we respect and say, "I believe in you." Between the lines we are saying, "I believe in what you are about, I have confidence in you and I'm with you."

Faith is not a set of beliefs to analyze, profess and defend with the threat of condemnation if someone disagrees. Tyranny has no place in love relationships or spirituality. It undermines both.

Beliefs can be helpful in getting me into my love affair with the Great I AM from which I can love others, but they are no substitute for it. If they don't serve to move me to where I experience The Living God's Love, they don't serve, or at least they need improvement.

Let's be careful about feeling absolutely right about any judgments of ourselves or others. There's always more going on than we can perceive as humans.

———

"Good" people of the world sometimes condemn parts of God without realizing it (and parts of themselves and others at the same time). This is a source of much unneeded pain.

———

Pray and play. Devotion to the Living God and playfulness go hand in hand. This is why Jesus said "unless you change and become like little children, you will never enter the kingdom of heaven." — Matthew 18:3 (NIV)

———

Our hearts yearn to be in a state of love with the Living God. Then we can reach out sincerely, lovingly, fairly and creatively with the Creative Love of God. Jesus did that at a miraculous level. That is a big part of why I follow him. I want my story to align with the Honest, Creative and Redeeming Love in his.

27

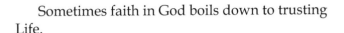

Sometimes faith in God boils down to trusting Life.

The right key is small but essential to a door. *The rest that works* has unlocked love when I couldn't otherwise. That's why Jesus invited us to value even a mustard-seed's worth of faith.

Trusting God has moved mountains in me.

Jesus was leading a different kind of revolution than anybody expected. It revolved around unlocking human hearts.

The ego tends to Edge God Out. Ironically, it's usually more out of fear than pride.

28

To worship is to earnestly value and honor as well as to want. It is not to place on a pedestal. Pedestals distance. They are a reverent way to avoid.

To truly love someone is to cherish them, want them and live accordingly. In this respect, it is the same with the Living God as with anyone else you know.

Our lives are aligned with what we truly worship.

The Bible makes clear what God considers worship: "(God) has shown you, O mortal, what is good. And what does the LORD require of you? To act justly and to love mercy and to walk humbly with your God" – Micah 6:8 (NIV).

Society's values can hinder the Loving Energies of God. Let's honor the latter first. Then we'll know how to beckon the best in society.

29

The Creative Forces of God are characterized by a passionate, loving desire. Cherish that Divine, Creative Energy in you.

Valuing love is part of worshipping God.

Our mindset alone can block our connection with God, reducing our perception of Divine Love to less than we can feel. *The rest that works* can change that.

Spiritually speaking, we tend to be a society of sleep-walkers. The irony is that resting our critical mind is often a prerequisite to waking-up.

Death never has the last word. The last word is not spoken here (if there even is such a thing).

ADAM AND EVE STUFF

"Congratulations to the one who stands at the beginning: that one will know the end and will not taste death." *(Jesus, the Gospel of Thomas, saying 18)**

It does not really matter if you take the story of Adam and Eve as fact or fable; its spiritual, psychological and social insights remain the same, and they are profound.

We often put inaccurate, judgmental expectations of God between us and the Living God. This is a huge problem that lies at the root of many if not most of our other issues.

* Translation by Stephen Patterson and Marvin Meyer.
http://gnosis.org/naghamm/gosthom.html

31

Anytime we see ourselves as fundamentally isolated from God we are somehow stuck in a psychological hiding place relative to Our Creator born of Adam and Eve stuff. If we truly live and move and have our being in God as the Bible says, it could not be otherwise (Acts 17:28).

———

Approaching God and people with a suspicious attitude is where a divisive condemning spirit can creep in like a venomous snake.

———

Everything changed as humans grasped for egocentric power through a spirit of self-justification and attack rather than Our Creator's Unconditional Love.

———

Judgments tend to block the flow of love. A judgmental attitude always does.

———

To be unconscious of our gift as co-creators with God results in thinking that we are going it alone; thinking so leads to experiencing life as such.

When we think we're alone relative to God, falling into Adam and Eve type fears and behaviors is almost unavoidable. Our vulnerability is so great.

The first step in returning to Paradise is earnestly wanting to leave the fame, blame and/or shame game behind.

We are usually unconscious of the ego dynamics driving us. *The rest that works* helps us not only become conscious; it helps us change the dynamics.

The Living God never expected us to be able to love unconditionally on our own.

Ego-centric approaches cannot work in the long run. They are forever insecure in being centered on a vulnerable, fearful self.

Ironically, we find ourselves by focusing on the Living God (in ourselves, others, the world and the Universe).

Genesis names loneliness as a fundamental human issue (Genesis 2:18). It also makes it clear that the Great I AM is ready to help us heal loneliness through loving relationships with God and others. (The gift of loneliness is that it helps us see how priceless home-making love is).

A condemning spirit kills from within no matter who's the target.

We become like the Push-Me-Pull-You animal of Dr. Dolittle fame when we try to worship both our ego and God.

It does not take making a statue to fall prey to the worst idolatry. Many people are on their knees in unhealthy and unnecessary ways without realizing it.

We don't grow by indirectly worshipping ourselves.

As chips off the ol' block of God, we experience our deepest identity through the free expression and reception of unconditional love; blocking it hurts because we are blocking our own true nature.

God created humanity to be wonderful co-creators with God in God. Since God is Love, we call upon the Creative Forces of God through loving.

There are powerful creative forces within us that stem from the Creative Forces of God. They want healthy, loving expression. Heavenly help can make all the difference (especially if we have pushed parts of ourselves down out of shame).

35

Allow the Living God. Simply allow.

It's great when my intellect and desire to love line-up (when I see exactly why and how I should love). But the faith that rescues and leads me home is trusting God and doing my best to love when I can't figure things out. *The rest that works* helps us do that.

Ask God to branch out through you with the kind of love that has made a difference for you.

Even when people fail, love's echoes remain. Listening for those echoes can help us hear the Living God in the here and now.

Attacking parts of ourselves rarely helps in the long run. When we attack, those parts usually retreat, only to emerge for a new round of conflict later.

36

Properly understood, the ego is a wonderful bud that has a valued place in the process of life.

A deep knowing is not characterized by feeling justified. It is characterized by the ego feeling blown away and relieved.

Family, health, sex, work and money create issues for everybody. Heaven is ready to help, starting from within.

The ego can also be seen as an I-piece at the end of a spyglass. Its main issues are clarity and focus on its true purpose – loving creatively with the Living God, no matter what issues are at hand.

The Adam and Eve story is mainly about how we hide parts of ourselves from God. Relief comes from doing the opposite. Give any things you hide to God (like sexual desires). You may be pleasantly surprised at what our Living, Loving Creator gives back. Our sexuality is meant to be a blessing, not a burden.

37

Our society worships practicality with the primary standard of worth being money. That costs too much when we dismiss unconditional love in the name of practicality. It can keep us from feeling and moving with the Redeeming (Revaluing) Love of God. We can pay a very high price.

Money is a medium of exchange. Let's fill its use with love and appreciation, not control or manipulation.

The pure, passionate love in our heart is holy, sacred stuff. It comes from the spark of God's Spirit in us. Honor it. Value it. See its worth. Fanning it into flame can change everything, starting with us.

The rest that works helps us stay positive, hopeful and creative as we discover things we don't like about ourselves and others. It makes correction and improvement possible where condemnation stopped loving growth before.

38

As we learn to trust in the Living God, we stay optimistic. God is ultimately working everything toward good (Romans 8:28). Our goal is to join in God's efforts.

Keep the goal in mind: Living in loving alignment with God.

Our Creator's Love involves a rich blending of the Masculine and Feminine Energies of Love (even in the Bible). Our lack of seeing and honoring that has hindered Christianity's ability to express love in keeping with the Holistic Love of God – not just toward women but nature and men as well. It has limited our ability to love anywhere near as expansively as God does.

Moving beyond patriarchal limitations is really about freeing the Great I AM from being relegated to a single image (valuable as that image is when healthy). It is to stop playing God with God. There is healthy freedom for everybody in that.

God honors us in allowing what we choose and always stands ready to help us make a better choice.

Divine Love means so much to us that there's really no comparison with anything else. We're not talking about comparing apples with oranges here. We're talking about comparing an orange with the state of Florida.

Sometimes, experience blows our limited functioning perspective out of the water. *The rest that works* helps us allow, accept and integrate such experiences. That's when the truth sets us free.

When the greatest experiences of Divine Love kick in, chances are you won't understand much. The euphoria will blow your mind. You will be utterly speechless other than repeating "Thank you." If you haven't experienced that yet, you have something wonderful to look forward to. From all I can tell, it's mainly a matter of sincerely practicing a complete yet personal form of *the rest that works* over time, embracing the changes it brings and passionately going after loving with God.

Don't say the miraculous is impossible (or it likely will be for you until you change your mind). God tends to honor our choices.

Let's have the humility to consider new evidence, the integrity to change our minds if facts challenge our assumptions and the courage to expand our thinking. That's how we grow.

Mystical experience often reveals that we've been living out of too small a framework. We realize that we haven't actually been open to what Jesus called the kingdom of God, or as I like to think of it, the "kindom" of God (which includes the Living God, Jesus and the Holy Spirit but also angels, great beings, saints, ancestors and deceased loved ones working with them).

Faith takes guts (mainly to break from social norms).

Some people do not take heavenly dimensions of reality seriously enough to experience the benefits of being open to them. They seal the door on the kingdom without even knocking on it (let alone paying attention to knocks from it).

The community made by the "kindom" of heaven bridges dimensions. This is why the Bible speaks of our being surrounded by a cloud of witnesses (Hebrews 12:1).

When we accept help from the "kindom" of heaven, we team-up across dimensions and help bring heavenly love to earth, one heart at a time. This is our true mission.

Living faithfully employs the Bible and other materials to orient us to God like a flower orients toward the sun. As God's Creative Love warms our hearts, growth and fruitfulness follow naturally.

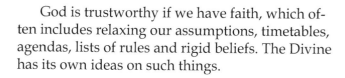

God is trustworthy if we have faith, which often includes relaxing our assumptions, timetables, agendas, lists of rules and rigid beliefs. The Divine has its own ideas on such things.

The rest that works is like a secret sauce that brings out the God Flavors of Life.

My heart wasn't just yanked out of my chest with the words, "Your daughter has a sarcoma." It felt like I dropped out of God's Hands, a place I'd felt secure most of my life. It took serious practicing of *the rest that works* to feel my way back there.

Nobody goes to hell without God going with them.

Some things are painful beyond our under-standing. Then the only peace that can come is peace that passes understanding — peace that comes in experiencing the flow of Divine Love in the midst of suffering. This is something the great saints have tried to convey and why Paul said to give thanks in all circumstances (1 Thessalonians 5:18).

Anxiety is contagious. Don't try to lessen it by giving it to others; that spreads dis-ease. Go to the Living God for healing and practice *the rest that works*.

If you catch anxiety from someone else, don't get mad at them. They're human. They simply caught a dis-ease. Go to God. The Living God can handle you and the situation, which includes lead-ing you in dealing with whatever is causing the dis-ease.

You are not just you. You stem from a much Larger, Unimaginably Incredible Being of Love. We get to be the cells and branches we are. We can settle into Divine Love and branch out with it. It's the opportunity of our lifetime.

44

ALIGNMENT

The Living God is already everywhere, but not everything moves in alignment with the Living God. Some things are characterized by contrast.

Alignment with the Living God was a very important issue to Jesus. One could argue that it was the most important issue to him.

The kingdom of heaven represents all that is in harmonized alignment with God, in this world and the next. To varying degrees, evil, hell and their counterparts represent serious misalignment (like cancer in a body).

We wouldn't drive a car that was seriously out of alignment, yet we often tolerate movements of spirit that are seriously out of alignment with Divine Love.

If we justify ourselves through blaming, shaming or putting someone else down, we might feel justified, but with what spirit have we aligned ourselves? (Not God).

Unconditional love is the best test of whether or not something is in alignment with God. Feel for it. When I can't feel it inside, I try to pause and follow *the rest that works* until I can. That assists my discernment of everything, inside and out.

Never squelch your desire to love. Re-orientation is the opposite of rejection. Re-alignment finds new ways to affirm the good and holy desires coming from the heart.

True alignment with God will not attack or drive any part of us to hide. Certain attitudes, desires and habits will fall away as that happen, but it is a healing, fruitful process.

＊

When I experience my dark side, I say something like this: "Most High God, please help me to see my selfish-ness and take responsibility for my part in what is off or wrong here. Correct me. Bring your energies in me into alignment with Your Love." Then I rest and try to get a feel for love and how to proceed.

REST (GRACE)

Relaxing is key to love getting through, both coming and going.

―∼―

The lizard-brain response to fearful things is a reactive fight or flight. *The rest that works* is a great tool for going deeper and aligning with God's Creative Love. It helps us move from being reactive to creative with the Greatest Forces in the Universe.

―∼―

Sabbath is about relaxing enough to allow God's Creative, Home-making Love to move in and through us. It's wise to do that at least a seventh of the time to stay spiritually healthy.

―∼―

The rest that works enables me to accept God's revaluing of me as priceless regardless of ways I "fail." As I stay true to the process, the peace of being at home with God starts coming from within and I can live in ways that work much better.

48

As we experience being in God's Hands, we realize Heaven is way ahead of us.

God has loving opportunities planned for everyone but the details are unique to each of us. That's why it is so important to develop our own personal form and practice of *the rest that works*.

When we hit a wall, we may need to step back to see the door or window God is opening. *The rest that works* helps us do that.

The unhealthy ego is like a bud that thinks the life of the branch is all about it. It needs perspective.

The ego has nothing to fear. A healthy branch does not kill its flowers. Life does not end as petals fall — it multiplies.

When it comes to getting lost, distractions can diffuse the power of God's Love in our life just as readily as fears and burdens can weigh us down.

⎯⎯⎯

We often follow our wants and fears oblivious to everything else, nibbling ourselves to nowhere. Then we look up and say, "How'd I get so lost?"

⎯⎯⎯

Freedom begins the moment we recognize unhealthy "self-ishness" and decide we don't want to let it govern how we do things anymore.

⎯⎯⎯

Releasing the desire of maintaining a self-image brings relief.

⎯⎯⎯

Over time, flexible masks can easily harden into brittle walls imprisoning the wearer.

⎯⎯⎯

No one feels at home where a judgmental, potentially condemning spirit governs. If it's in us, we cannot find a home anywhere because we do not even feel safe with ourselves. *The rest that works* allows God in to clean house.

Sometimes we want to love but there are blocks in us. We have the will but we can't find a way. *The rest that works* is the best way I have found to relax and release internal blockage.

Fear assuaged by success is not the same as fear erased by grace: The former may only expand or improve a prison. The latter removes walls.

Grace is the best way to relieve tension and remove strings. It opens avenues for much better relationships (with the least pain).

Guilt is one of the heaviest burdens we ever carry, especially when legitimate. That's why coming to the Living God and coming clean are so important. God always responds to that approach with Grace and opportunity.

—◆—

We are wise to resist the urge to justify ourselves. Otherwise, we might justify ourselves with something other than God's Love. Keep doing it and we could get stuck somewhere we don't want to be. The Living God's Love needs no justification or defense.

—◆—

Grace brings mercy and truth together in miraculous ways.

—◆—

The biggest single recurring problem we have is people not taking responsibility for their underlying intentions and the spirit with which they pursue them. Let's make sure we do so. That's one of the best gifts we can give the world (and ourselves).

—◆—

To repent is to rethink (be re-pensive) and say "God, please align my heart with Your's again." The goal is not to get off the hook. The goal is to get ourselves in right alignment and work from there.

The rest that works helps us move with our wild and passionate yet always loving soul – the spark of the Great I AM in us.

We need to let go of some of the ways we evaluate ourselves and others through society's notions of good and evil. As we do so, we discover that what was anticipated as a painful loss is actually liberating and exhilarating.

Letting go sets free.

If conflict lasts more than a half-hour, ego and self-esteem are almost surely involved. Ask God for help in those areas, especially for you personally (you have no control of others).

53

See mistakes, try to learn from them, try to make things right and go on. Skip a condemning spirit. You can simply skip it.

Before arguing anything, ask yourself: What's my real goal here? Am I really trying to secure my ego?

We can only enjoy ourselves without reservation when our sense of self-worth rests securely in God's Hands.

The rest that works enables us to accept necessary losses with grace rather than resentment.

Love prayerfully – then don't worry about what people think of you. (They will think you're crazy sometimes).

The first step toward improving our relationships is to remove the reasons others might fear
us.

When you realize that God is doing psychological work with you, take off your inner shoes - you
are standing on holy ground. Honor the Living
God as heaven teaches you about you.

There is usually a valid, natural root to our desires. Needed corrections are usually a matter of
letting selfish elements fall off of otherwise healthy
desires.

We cannot condemn anyone without condemning a part of God. Let's aim at correction
rather than condemnation. Containment is often a
valid step of correction. (It's why we have Depart-
ments of Corrections).

55

Street-wisdom involves being cautious while staying present and open to possibilities. This helps explain why Jesus said be innocent as doves but wise as serpents (Matthew 10:16).

Mutual assessment sets the stage of most social interactions. It can be hard to break through the acting that ensues. It's up to us to see what's happening and relax our personal masks.

Mutual safety is necessary for any true intimacy.

Evaluation stalks us. It's how we organize ourselves. It's how we manage things. We must assess some things in order to be good stewards of life and the world. But when a critical, condemning spirit gets involved — a spirit that would put down without lifting up — watch out. Divine Love does not work like that. The most serious problems are not solved that way; they are created.

Grace can change everything when deep love fills a spot where condemnation has a right to be. This is why "Father forgive them, they know not what they do" echoes from the cross after 2,000 years.

A big part of *the rest that works* is taking responsibility for our stuff. Another big part is taking our stuff to the Living God. There is no need to try to handle anything without God.

We are wise to question our questions. Try not to ask any unless you know the true spirit behind them. Articulate only those questions aligned with love. Be impeccable in this and your life will change because people will truly be safe with you.

The hardest thing is cowering in shame or fear before ourselves. Sometimes we need Heavenly Help to dismiss the condemning spirit in us.

The inner critic isn't wise enough to play judge. His method can identify blockages but by itself it can't move us toward the ultimate goal – living in redeeming, creative love. That kind of love isn't trying to nail anything down. It is trying to free.

It's best if the inner critic can evolve into a wise, loving coach.

WORK

I pray to the Living God every time I think of it. That hasn't been a mistake yet, especially when heaven has led me to others (or to fix things like a leaky toilet).

The rest that works is not simply about rest. It's also about renewal and a resurgence of life. It's about roots and wings.

As we learn how to rest in the Home-making Love of God, we can let go of a lot of distractions, dead-ends, meaningless debates and fears of daily life. It's amazing how much space that creates.

All the Holy Spirit really needs to work miracles is a heart open to love that wants to love (which includes our personal passions as well as other people).

59

Respect is the first step of home-making love. When respect isn't the undergirding movement of spirit, we can spend all sorts of effort and never get where we want to go. Respect lays the essential foundation we want.

As we have concrete experiences of God's Home-making Love, worry loses its grip on us. We're at home as we go.

Living in harmony with Divine Love does not lead to weakness. It leads to responsible empowerment as branches of The Divine. It works to bring what we really want – a deep sense of wellbeing from within.

The answer to a problem is often not to pull back but to move forward creatively. *The rest that works* helps us see what kind of action is needed.

Take the risk of loving unconditionally with God. It's worth it (and it's usually more fun)!

Avoid games that de-value people. The price is always too high.

It is the love behind an act that counts. Love welcomes God.

Like a cell in a body is not just a cell but an integral part of a body, you are not just you. You are an integral part of the Living God in which we live and move and have our being. There's amazingly good news in that.

A good prayer anytime is: "Loving God in me, please align the rest of me with You." Then feel for sincere, creative love and move with it.

61

Life is already eternal. Death is simply a doorway to where we are really at (spiritually).

———〜—

Living *the rest that works* doesn't mean we will escape experiences in the world that scare us, but it frees us from bowing to fear or playing the attacking-blame-and-shame game.

———〜—

When considering anything ask: "What's the spirit behind this?"

———〜—

When it comes to specifics, there are as many paths as people. But the pattern, the way home with God is going to involve love.

———〜—

Sometimes, we must rest regarding our ability to sort out a mess and simply keep working the best we know out of love. We can rest in the knowledge that God can always work with that.

———〜—

Unconditional Love ignores social evaluations except to gain insight into suffering.

Avoid a business approach to spiritual things (which includes people); the style of questioning itself will most likely cheapen things, including you. Approach people like the treasure they are. Remember, lost treasure is still treasure.

Jesus re-valued everybody. He invited people to return home to God by accepting that God treasured them and everybody else. He invited people to respond by treasuring God and each other.

Commit not to toss any babies out with bath-water (much better to keep both if you can't separate a baby safely – what's a little dirt compared to a baby?). There is a precious child of God in all people, no matter how hidden.

Like God and Jesus used the cross, Grace and Divine Love can put evil to work in new ways. Crosses become tools in God's Hands when we live *the rest that works*.

When we say "God is Love," we aren't talking about touchy-feely, happy-go-lucky love. We are talking about Love so powerful and creative that it births stars and turns instruments of death into beacons of Light. God's Love is powerful stuff.

The rest that works helps us to be true to how God created us rather than some trumped-up image. There is deep relief in being ourselves.

The business of the soul isn't calculated, it's born. The experience is birthed of wondrous love; pure, unadulterated love. Let such love be and holiness will fill your heart - like when staring into a beautiful baby's eyes in wonder after the miracle of birth.

Heaven guides us in how to love and get needed things done when we live *the rest that works*.

———

Make space for the holy. Simply let it be (especially when you feel it in you). That will help you see and honor it in others.

———

Whatever we do to anyone we do to God – not to God's entirety but to a part of the Living God.

———

The spark of Our Creator's "I AM" Spirit inside each of us has come on a mission to shine in this challenging world. To the degree we leave our windows dirty, we experience drudgery without light. To the degree we polish our inner windows so that our light can shine, we find meaning in the labors of life. Life is invigorating as we feel our soul's mission is being accomplished.

———

Any sincere love can connect us with Divine Love. It may need some improvement, but that's probably all it needs.

It's hard to love creatively. Our fears are so many. But as we experience the Hand of Heaven in our lives, we start to trust the Living God to handle us and our part in any situation.

We are adventurers who have branched out into a leading edge dimension of creation. God would not have let us do that without significant means of support. *The rest that works* is a way to tap into heavenly and worldly support.

The issues between us are usually more about conflicting choices than our fundamental identity. We are all children of God. Our conflicts come from various degrees of human confusion and choices that miss the mark of loving.

Communion isn't so much about the sacrament shared in worship services (although the Eucharist can give us a taste of the real thing). It's about living in God's Love with Jesus and others. That kind of communion leads to experiencing our deep oneness as children of God.

66

We share our deepest identity.

Alive in God's Love, we realize that whenever anyone does evil they are lost, especially to themselves. We need not employ a condemning spirit toward them to take a stand against what they are doing. To stop them is sometimes the most respectful thing we can do, but we can do so with compassion and a hope of appealing to their true, better nature as the child of God they really are. (This also applies to us).

If love that values souls isn't getting through, rest. Take a break. Pause and pray about it. In this way we can open to guidance and make sure that we are offering the respectful love we want. We cannot dishonor someone without dishonoring ourselves.

We all lie at Mother Nature's breast. As humans, "we live and move and have our being" in God by way of Mother Nature (Acts 17:28). We have done a very poor job of honoring Mom.

67

Egocentricity as an orientation has entered into a period of judgment in the 21st century. Our judge isn't so much a God of anthropomorphic imagination as an Earthly reality.

Mother Nature cannot afford to let us keep acting like spiritual two-year olds, both for Her sake but also Her future children's sake (including our grandchildren).

Adore Mother Nature again like you did as a little child.

The key to our environmental challenges is to work with the Creative Forces of God as revealed in Mother Nature and in us. Get to know yourself as organically as possible. The Living God will lead you in this if you will let God.

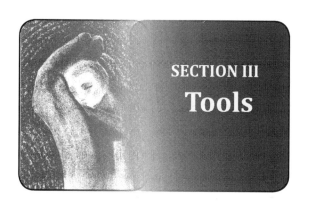

SECTION III
Tools

*"Prayer doesn't change
God. Prayer changes me."*
– C. S. Lewis

PRAYER NAPS

When I ask myself, what habit has made the biggest difference in my life, the answer is simple — prayer naps; my version of meditative prayer. Other habits and tools help a lot, like paying attention to significant dreams and signs. The big book on *the rest that works* and other materials offer tools and approaches for those, but if you were going to do just one thing, I'd say "Develop some type of consistent, open-ended prayer." Consistently give Heaven a sincere, relaxed opportunity to get through to you with love and if necessary, guidance.

I try to commit at least 30 minutes a day to a prayer nap. I sit in a chair or lie down and sincerely open to God. I take some deep breaths and relax, coming back to an open intent before God as long as I stay conscious. If I fall asleep, I don't worry about it (though if I'm super tired, I'll intentionally lay with the goal of falling asleep). Settling in with the Love of the Living God is the goal of a prayer nap. I try to do it at least once a day, for real. Sometimes days go by between times. Okay. It doesn't matter how long it's been. If I think about it, I try to do it. No beating up; simply get back to it.

The first five seconds usually go pretty well. After that anything's possible. Sometimes thoughts come like crazy. Sometimes there's just a trickle. Sometimes pretty much nothing happens and I simply get up relaxed, trusting that's fine. Sometimes there are visions and things that turn out to be meaningful communication. In terms of the practice, it doesn't matter. The task is the same: return daily to sincere, open intent before God. Commit the time (at bare minimum 15 minutes). Sincerely offering ourselves to the Living God is worth it.

Distractions abound during a prayer nap, inside and out. The phone may ring. If you can, let it go. You can call them back in half an hour. The thoughts in our heads are the more difficult distractions. Many of them make legitimate points: "Gotta do this. . . gotta do that. . ." You can leave a notepad by the chair to jot things down for the first few minutes so long as you commit to let that go at some point. You can always make a list when you're done. Things tend to come up again later anyway, but nothing is more important than your relationship with the Living God. If practicality leads you to question the value of this practice, answer the question: "The Source of Life is worth more than any thing in life. You can afford to invest in creating a channel for the Living God to reach you, love you and work through you." Ignore the fact that society does not encourage this. Have the courage to do it. Even if nothing perceptible happens, you are honoring the Living God. Over time, Spirit will work with that.

Whatever you do, don't beat yourself up if you experience an uncontrollable "monkey mind," as the Buddha called it. Laugh about it if that happens (which it probably will on and off forever). Don't try to force the monkey down. Instead, give it a banana and invite it to rest or swing in the trees. Play with the situation. The Living God likes creative play, like that of a parent with an adored young child. Correction may come, but if we are open, it will come in that positive spirit.

A lot of observation occurs in the first few minutes of a prayer nap. Sometimes we simply need to let thoughts come and go. That's natural and still happens for me after years of practice. Let them come and go like clouds through the sky or boats floating down a river. Don't let them hijack you off the bank. You don't need to jump on every passing boat. Have fun waving to the passengers and wishing them well as they go by! Give them

all to God as you are open to spiritual guidance.
This time is between you and the Living God. It
is not greedy to honor this time. It is spiritually
healthy and actually one of the most responsible
things you can do. Strengthening your relationship
with the Living God will empower your ability to
respond to others with genuine unconditional love
rather than egocentric fears and agendas. It may
be the best gift you ever give.

Knowing that the Living God is with you, seek
to be with God. Ask God to run the experience
and relax. Be mindful that God is in you as well
as around you. Take responsibility for your part,
which is to rest in knowing that you exist as an expression or breath of God, The Great I AM Within
all Life. Rest in knowing that you are a branch of
a beautiful Vine; rest in knowing that you are like
a cell in a wonderful, loving body. The ultimate
goal of the prayer nap isn't to get God moving
with us, that's already happening; it is to get us
moving more in sync with the Living God and the
unforced rhythms of Grace.

We're like cells with God's DNA of Divine
Love, but also with our God-given free will. Sometimes we are going in the exact opposite direction
of God mentally and behaviorally. As we feel the
influence of or get caught in the downward spiral
of the judgmental or critical spirit, we spin in an
opposite direction of the freeing, uplifting swirl
of God's Grace. Consciously moving with God's

Uplifting Love is the ultimate goal of practicing *the rest that works* in all we do, including meditative practice.

Taking a prayer nap now

Let me say one thing for anyone who might be feeling a little anxiety as I invite opening up to God more deeply in a few moments. A wise old pastor once told me, "Sometimes anxiety comes from proximity to God." We intuitively know that opening ourselves to the Living God is potentially big stuff. If you are feeling anxious, my guess is that you may be feeling some of this natural anxiety. It invites a healthy respect for God, but there is no need to be afraid of God or heavenly beings. They are always behind us. And it's always a mystery as to how God works. I still get a little anxious and excited when I feel Divine Energy rising in me. But it's good energy, like a kid feels in a candy store. It's merely hard for us to sense or experience it, especially if we have been following our fears, been distracted, are in poor health or circumstances are difficult. The Living God understands all of that. God and heavenly beings might very well encourage a change in perspective or behavior, but that is because God is with us, wanting what is truly best for us and for others.

Back to technique in a prayer nap: Once I'm open to the Living God behind my being alive, I might pay attention to my breathing patterns and rhythmically say to myself things like "in with Your Love," and "out with Your Grace." This method can be very helpful because we often need God's Grace, for us and for others. A more basic pattern is "In You," and "With You"—like a drop being thankful for becoming aware of the ocean.

Soon, I'm not really thinking about breathing at all but feeling a spiritual shift and a sense of relief in God's Life-giving Love. I often drop any attempt to stay conscious of the pattern of breathing at this point and simply seek to move in the moment with God. Does it mean that I know God's Will in that moment? Probably not. I give God thanks for creating me and for my experiential awareness of somehow being part of the Living God in whom "we live and move and have our being" (Acts 17:28, NIV). As cognition gives way to sensation and a deeper "knowing," the Holy Spirit gives peace that passes understanding.

Sometimes we feel a surge of energy move through us unexpectedly, as something wonderful stirs in us when we witness a loving act in life or even a movie. The sensation reminds us of the Love at work in the world that lurks beneath the surface, giving life. This breathing exercise gives a simple way to have the tiniest, intentionally conscious experience of that Life-giving Love. By focusing on Life itself, we can connect with the Divine, Creative Forces behind it.

During a prayer nap, don't let words remain

76

mere ideas in your head. As you think phrases like "Your Love," recognize God as you might recognize a wonderful, loving relative. As the shift happens for you, it will probably feel more humbling than that, but that's a good sign. Then trust God's Unconditional Love for you. If you feel yourself questioning God's Love for you, remind yourself that God — The Spirit Behind and Within all Life — is already giving you life unconditionally. The fact that you are here proves it. As that truth sinks in, let it lift you. We can feel so much more than fear. We can live in faith and feel the fruits of it. We can trust Love to find or create a way forward, no matter what. As we move deeper with that, moving beyond a mere physical and mental exercise, the shift can open a wellspring that lifts our spirits like buoyant water floats bubbles.

Don't worry if you feel energy moving in you, in your chest, in your hands, on the top of your head, or up and down your spine. Focus on God's Love more and move with the energy. These sensations remind me of when Jesus said, "Whoever has will be given more and he will have an abundance. Whoever does not have, even what he has will be taken from him" (Matthew 13:12, NIV). Jesus' words don't mean that a jealous God takes back what isn't appreciated, but that we receive more spiritual energy as we learn how to receive it. As we tap into the wellspring of God's Love, more of God's Loving Energy becomes available,

77

especially if we are seeking to flow with it towards someone else. God wants to both love us and love through us. That's God's Plan. It's what Jesus was talking about when he talked about letting our light shine.

Abundance is exactly what I experience spiritually as I increase my awareness of the Living God and seek to participate in God's Loving. Sometimes I sense more Loving Energy available than I could ever hold. I realize that I have been taking an eyedropper to a vast ocean. Now I understand that a faucet exists within me and all I need to do is open the valve. As a faith stance and practice, *the rest that works* puts my hand on the handle. Moments of actual personal prayer turn it.

I say prayers as long as I feel they are helpful, and then I try to move into not thinking any words at all. Then it is just a matter of breathing and identifying with the Larger Life that is living through me. I look out of my eyes, trying not to merely identify with "Scott Daniels" but the Larger Being who is looking through my eyes. This Being is "God with us" of whom I am a branch, as we all are. My sense of self relaxes in these moments and I usually feel more energy in my hands or tingles in my back. I experience that I am a being that is focused through my body, but not just my body. I realize that I am using a mind to process what is being seen and felt through my body, but that I am more truly the being who is choosing between

78

thoughts than the mind that is developing them. The mind becomes the tool that it is rather than the taskmaster it thinks it should be. That's liberating.

God loves you with the kind of love symbolized by the child in God's Hand on the cover of this book. My brother, John, sketched that, inspired by Isaiah 49:16: "I have inscribed you on the palms of my hands." I've had it on my desk for years to remind me of how God loves me and everyone. I also remind myself that aligning with a hand as powerful as that can work in ways I could never achieve alone.

Prayer renders its greatest gifts over time. Deepening our experience of God through the kind of practices outlined here offers a lifetime opportunity. Seize it day by day. God wants you to accept it and will help you do so in the way that is right for you, if you allow the Living God to lead your life

REST STOP

"Find a quiet, secluded place so you won't be tempted to role-play before God. Just be there as simply and honestly as you can manage. The focus will shift from you to God, and you will begin to sense his grace."
—Jesus in Matthew 6:6 (MSG)

Let me invite you to take a prayer nap now. Please make yourself comfortable. Use some light, meditative music and candles if you wish. Your intent: to relax and be open to God. Settle in with Divine Love — the love that is already giving you life. Don't worry if nothing seems to happen. Trust that the intent is enough. The Living God will work with it over time if you keep giving God time.

Once you are comfortable, say something to God like, "Lord, I open myself to You, asking for Your protection and guidance at this time. Thank You for my angels and the heavenly beings who are working with me. Thank You for the people in my life. Help me do what is the most loving and of the highest good toward them and toward myself. Please draw me into alignment with You, Your Love and Your Will." (I also raise any recent dreams or potential signs for understanding and direction with an open heart and mind.) Then relax, coming back to that open intent as long as you stay conscious. If you fall asleep, don't worry about it. In fact, trust God to work with that too. Maybe you needed a nap! Good. That may be the best thing at this time.

FREEING A MASTERPIECE

When asked how he created such masterpieces as his statue of David, Michelangelo said the masterpiece was already in the marble. He simply set it free.

The rest that works is a tool for placing yourself in God's Hands and working with the Master, step by step. It yields it's best work over time.

Just as Michelangelo needed the marble to stay at rest relative to him, we need to do so relative to God in order for the Holy Spirit to reveal and develop the masterpieces we really are. We need to come to peace with our soul—the spark of the Great I AM in us—so unhelpful self-images, habits and ways of thinking can drop off. We need to let go of some of the ways we use to evaluate ourselves and others through society's notions of good and evil. As we do so, we discover that what was anticipated as painful is actually liberating and exhilarating. Our true self is set free.

The material we have put between us and the Living God often has to be chipped away bit by bit. That's usually how those layers got there – following our fears bit by bit rather than moving in faith. Unloving habits created a mask confusing us and our relationships with God and others. Heaven wants to remove those layers without hurting us. *The rest that works* is a way to test for love, let the chips fall where they may and offer the best of ourselves to the Living God and the world.

More power to you masterpiece.

Blessings,
Scott

82

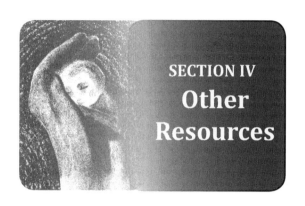

SECTION IV
Other Resources

"We live and move and have our being in God. God lives and moves and seeks expression in all of Creation, including us."

This book is a publication of RTW Press, part of the multi-faceted ministry of The Rest that Works, LLC, aimed at helping people rest in God so they can work and play from there.

On our website (theresthatworks.com), you will find a blog and other items to support people in living *the rest that works*. Resources include:

- the main text on *the rest that works* (sometimes known as the Big Book),
- items for personal journaling and dream-work,
- guided meditations (available as download-able mp3's),
- worship materials, and
- videos and other materials for classes and small groups

You also will find information about an online coaching program for individuals (which can include coaching with the author by phone).

Additional copies of this book (and the Big Book) can be obtained at Amazon.com, Rider Green Books and other retail outlets. To inquire about volume discounts (five or more copies) write info@ridergreen.com. (All materials are copyrighted by Scott Daniels and The Rest that Works, LLC).

NOTES

Made in the USA
Middletown, DE
04 September 2016